CODING

BASICS FOR BEGINNERS

THE SMART WAY TO APPROACH
THE WORLD OF COMPUTER PROGRAMMING
AND THE FUNDAMENTAL FUNCTIONS
OF THE MOST POPULAR LANGUAGES SUCH AS

PYTHON, JAVA AND C++

JEFFERSON SANDYMAN

TABLE OF CONTENT

Introduction

So, you're interested in learning to code but don't know where to start? This book is going to be your one-stop shop for everything coding. We will give you a brief overview of what coding is and how it can make a difference in any industry, then we'll go into why it's essential for everyone from high school students to seniors. We'll also provide some resources on learning for free and teaching yourself more advanced skills on your own time.

What is coding?

Coding is the process where you put instructions into a particular computer language. The computer can understand this code, and the code can control how the computer functions, which in turn helps people, accomplish their goals. Coding is one of the fastest-growing and highest-paying jobs in America. (Bureau of Labour Statistics, 2015) If you've ever used an ATM or used a credit card to pay for something, coding was used to help make that happen.

How does it work?

A programmer writes code using special programs on your computer keyboard or a text editor, such as Notepad on Windows or TextEdit on OS X. The code tells the computer what to do or how to function, like the instructions on a piece of paper that you are writing. This code can help a person do anything that requires programming skills like making games, connecting electronic devices, programming robots, and so much more.

Why is it important?

Programming skills are essential in every industry. Many jobs in technology require coding such as software engineers, technicians, and IT specialists. Even more than these jobs, other positions in tech fields don't have programming skills at

—

all but instead require expertise in specific programs and languages. In schools, coding is often used to teach students all the skills needed for success in many different industries. Coding can give students the experience they need to make something happen, learn how to be independent and creative, and work well under pressure. It's nothing to be afraid of; it's just programming!

Where can I learn?

There are plenty of resources out there on the internet to get you started. There are many resources available online for free or for a small fee, such as Codecademy, Code Academy, Lynda.com, and Udemy. You may even want to try your own hands at creating code from scratch - you might have some ideas already. All you need is a computer, an internet connection, and some motivation.

Code your goals!

This is only the beginning of where coding can take you in your life! You'll be able to use this knowledge to learn more advanced skills that will have more meaning for you on your own time - teaching yourself how to use more advanced software languages like C++ or Python. Maybe you'll become a web designer and create your sites or applications to help you learn more about your skills. This is the time of your life - take it!

Coding is just a small step in the larger technology industry, and anyone can take that step with you. It's truly as fun as it sounds and will teach you things that can be applied throughout life. If you're ready to dive in, we'll see you there!

Chapter 1.

Common Terms and Their Definition

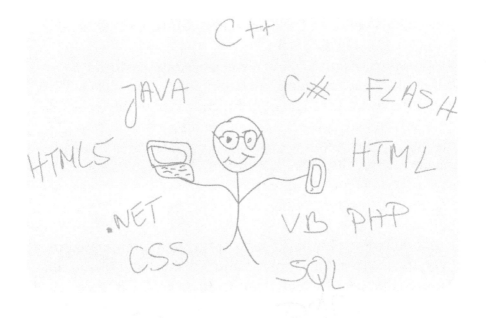

Coding: Converting a problem into code, or a string of symbols and language that a computer can process.

HTML: Hypertext markup language, or how the information on your site is presented to users. HTML is used for formatting text, pictures, links, video, and audio.

JavaScript: A programming language used for web development makes it easier to build interactive websites and add effects like scrolling boxes and drop-down menus. JavaScript allows you to create more dynamic pages that work faster than the static pages produced from pure HTML can achieve.

Node.js: A JavaScript framework that allows you to build powerful real-time applications using an event-driven and non-blocking I/O model.

jQuery: A JavaScript library that simplifies HTML document traversing, event handling, animating, and Ajax interactions for rapid web development.

Responsive Design: Making a website adapt its design to different screen sizes (smartphones, tablets, laptops, etc.) without affecting the layout or functionality of the website.

Test-Driven Development: Automated software testing method or framework based on creating test cases from an incomplete specification. It asserts that developers should specify code before writing it.

Basic words used in coding.

1. Abbreviation: Shortened form of text or a group of words. Everyday use is to give organizations a short and memorable name so that people can remember them easily. It is also used as an informal way to express complicated concepts or ideas by using only some part of the whole world, which helps save time when reading the abbreviation and typing it. For example, "Max" in "Maxwell" can also be used to describe a variable in math formulas, and similarly, "X1000" may be describing a million (1000x) rather than being an actual number (1x1000).

2. Accessibility: The ease of accessing content on a website or other media. Many different aspects make up a website's accessibility, including design, content, and technology.

3. API: Application programming interface. A set of routines, protocols, and tools for building software applications

4. Cache: Temporary storage available on the web browser of your computer or mobile device that stores data in a faster or more efficient manner than it is retrieved from the site itself. It allows the browser to load websites more quickly by storing commonly accessed web page elements like text, graphics, and sounds. Caching also enables users to access online information even if there is no Internet connection available at the time.

4. Challenge-response authentication: A type of security protocol where a user is first challenged to provide some information about them and then presented with a response calculated on that original information that they must enter or re-enter to proceed.

5. Character encoding: The mechanism for representing textual data by converting it into a sequence of (usually) 8-bit characters using an alphabet and/or character set.

6. Command line: In computing, command lines are a text-based way to communicate with a computer's operating system, programs, and applications through typed commands. It is mainly used for programming or performing simple tasks like compiling code or opening programs on the command line instead of using the mouse or graphical interfaces.

7. Configuration: The process of identifying and defining settings that a device communicates with when operating.

8. CYA: (Also known as CAPS) Courtesy, yet another acronym meant all the above. It is often used in user interface design.

9. Contextual Accessibility: The ease by which a person can gain access to content on a website or other media, given its

current context (location, time, task). Contextual accessibility is about recognizing the context in which people are using technology at any given moment of their lives while they're online and using it to meet their needs appropriately – according to their current needs and interests.

10. Digital Divide: The gap between individuals, households and communities that have access to the internet and the digital resources available online, and those that does not.

11. Encoding: The method in which information is converted into strings of symbols can be transmitted, stored or processed by a computer. A common example of encoding is ASCII, representing text as a sequence of numbers ranging from 0 to 255.

12. File Extension: The suffix at the end of a file name after the period/dot symbol (ex: .html). It identifies what type of file it is like .html for HTML files.

13. Globalization: The process of adapting content (including, but not limited to, information and software) from one language and cultural context to another.

15. Hyperlink: A type of reference (a link) between two or more locations on the same site. Usually, a hyperlink will open either a new window or new tab in a web browser that reads the referenced text or image at that location.

15. Internet Explorer: A series of graphical user interface (GUI) web browsers developed by Microsoft for Windows systems that support HTML 4 and CSS 2 selectors and ActiveX controls.

16. Internet search engine: A form of web search that does not directly retrieve text data from a specific source but instead

searches the entire World Wide Web for documents that contain the relevant keywords and returns those that are most likely to include this information.

17. JavaScript: A programming language designed by Netscape and first released in 1995. It is an object-oriented scripting language that can be embedded into client-side web pages or as standalone programs, which creates interactive experiences on the client-side of the browser.

18. Java: (JavaScript) is a programming language that enables developers to write dynamic web pages and applications and run them inside a browser.

19. Macro: Computer code that is executed automatically when some other code is triggered by the user by using hotkeys in a word processing program or by pressing a button on a mouse. Some macro features come built into certain operating systems (e.g., Microsoft Office, Apple iTunes, Mac OS X). In computer aided design (CAD) software, macros are used to automate repetitive tasks in the software so that fewer mouse movements or keystrokes are required.

Chapter 2.

What Is a Programming Language?

The first thing you need to know is that a programming language is a set of instructions for the computer. These are often called code. The goal is to make computers do what they need to do, ranging from making calculators to processing NASA images of nearby galaxies. But the hard part about programming languages is that they're often not designed for people who don't already know how to program. It's like trying to teach someone Spanish in a first-grade class. Most people aren't going to be able to understand what you're saying.

That's why this book is for absolute beginners who don't know any programming languages at all. It doesn't matter how much experience you have in other languages; you'll still need basic knowledge of computers to pick up this language and use it effectively. (If you want more information about these topics, check out my other books on web development.)

What Is Coding?

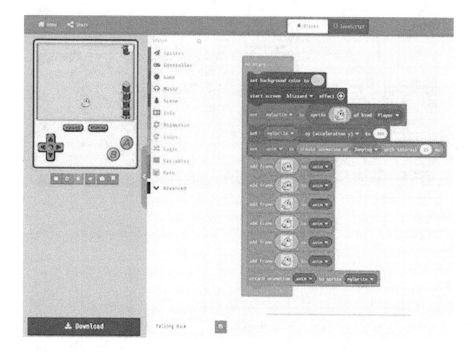

You can think of code as instructions that tell the computer what to do. If I say to the computer, "draw a picture," it will draw a picture on the screen. The laptop has a great deal of programming power built into it, including the ability to understand instructions. It might have to make a little interpretation on one or two of them, but for the most part, it can follow these instructions and do what you ask.

Why Do We Code?

Programming languages are used to make software. Software is vital because it lets us do things like automate processes in factories or connect devices in our homes to control them from anywhere else in the world. This kind of software is commonly called "apps," short for applications.

So coding is necessary because it gives us the ability to make apps of our own to help us do what we want. But coding is more than just the language: it's about what you can do with that language.

Coding is also a creative process, and that's where all the best apps come from. Successful apps are those that are useful, interesting, or just downright fun to use. Some of them have changed how we live our lives, like Uber or Facebook; others have profoundly affected how we communicate with each other, like Skype or WhatsApp. And they've all been made possible because someone somewhere had an idea and was able to translate it into code.

What Can You Do with It?

Anything you can think of. Coding gives you the ability to make something out of nothing. You give it a few lines of code and it turns into a program that does something on your computer, across your network, or even the World Wide Web. You might think that all coding is the same, but there are several different kinds. Some coding languages are used to build simple websites. Others are used to build operating systems, which makes them complicated. Some people learn how to write code in high school or college to write programs for big companies like Google and Microsoft; others learn how to code for themselves or their friends to make their software without much money.

Here in this book, you're going to learn how to build software for your computer using a popular programming language called Python. This is a great language to learn because there are lots of resources out there for learning it. There are also lots of apps out there that were made using Python so you can see how they work, play with them, and even copy them to use as your projects.

You might think that some of these websites and apps cost money or require special equipment, but all you need is a computer. And right now, that's all you need to learn to code : just a computer with an internet connection and the ability to read, type, and do some simple math.

How to Read This Book

Programming is a complicated subject. Even if you're entirely new to computers, it's pretty likely you already know at least some programming languages. That's why I wrote this book so that people who have no experience coding can still understand what they're reading. Here are the steps you need to take to use this book:

1. Download and install Python 2 on your computer if you don't already have it installed. (Python 3 is very similar and many of the examples will work with either version.)

2. Open a web browser on your computer and enter this address: https://codecademy.com/courses/learn-python?action=start.

3. Follow along as you read the chapters. You should type in the code and follow the instructions for each chapter. (If you don't see any code or instructions, then click "Start a new lesson.")

4. Continue with this book until the end. You'll want to practice what you learn so that it sticks in your memory!

Where to Learn More

Once you finish this book, you're going to want to learn more about Python and coding. Here are some resources I recommend:
Codecademy – Codecademy is an interactive website where you can learn how to code in dozens of languages, including Python, by completing activities and challenges on their platform. They even have video tutorials!
Codecademy is an interactive website where you can learn how to code in dozens of languages, including Python, by completing activities and challenges on their platform. They even have video tutorials! Udacity.

This is like Codecademy, except it's a college level course and the program you learn here can be applied to most jobs. The site also has many videos showing you how the modules work and how to use them. Books and YouTube – These are two great ways to learn, and they're all free! You can learn Python through many books or online courses. You can also search YouTube videos on Python to see how people have used it in their projects.

Chapter 3.

Why Do We Need a Programming Language?

The most common use for a computer is to store and retrieve data. Computers can read information stored on the memory chips and turn it into text, video, or any other format that we can view. However, they cannot understand or process the information itself—it's just a bunch of electronic impulses. So what does that mean? It means that it needs us, humans, to tell it what to do for the computer to do anything at all. Now, this is where programming languages come in handy because they enable us, humans, to tell computers how to process the data we store on them. Yes, this does require us to know how to write a program that tells the computer what to do. However, writing a program by hand isn't an option if we want the computer to do anything! Computers can only operate in eight different modes; they can only understand English or binary code.

So we need a way for computers to understand and process human languages of all kinds. Programming languages have been developed so that anyone with minimal training can write programs — everything from simple webpages and word processors to complex games like Quake III Arena and World of Warcraft. It is the same type of language used in everything from chat rooms and music players on our computers to mobile phones and digital cameras. If you want to move beyond just writing small programs for your use, you will need to learn how to program to create the software that makes all this possible.

How to explain Coding to a kid?

Programming is making choices about what data the computer should process to achieve the desired result. There are many kinds of programming languages, some more complicated than others, but all have something in common. They all require us to choose a set of instructions that tell the computer exactly how we want it to operate. Sounds simple — it is!

Let's look at an example: You have just bought an iPod and want it to play music from your computer via iTunes. You have a couple of songs stored on your computer's hard drive, but you want it to take those songs and play them over the iPod. How do you tell iTunes to do this? Just plug in the iPod and select it from iTunes' menu, right? Well, that works — but maybe you want to think about what is even happening here.

If the only thing we know is that we need iTunes to transfer songs into our iPod, then why aren't we just hooking up our computer directly via USB instead?

If we start thinking like a programmer here, we can see some choices we need to make. First of all, we have to decide which songs we want to transfer over. Second, we need to tell iTunes that those are the songs that we want it to transfer over. And third, iTunes needs to know how we want it to transfer them — iPod or computer?

How do you do this? Well, iTunes is a relatively simple program that the user can easily control with just a few clicks of a mouse. However, underneath this easy-to-use interface is a somewhat more complex set of instructions that tell iTunes exactly how to work. This is what programming languages do for computers — they let us type out those instructions and then translate them into the commands the computer can understand and process.

What's Coding Like?

Programming is not the same as just typing in lots of random numbers and letters. Instead, it can be a bit like solving a puzzle. You are trying to figure out how to tell the computer what you want it to do, without relying on knowing how all of that stuff works — just like solving a puzzle!

So what are some examples of coding problems that you might come across? Well, computers use different types of data that they need to process according to their programming language. For example, some computers will have straightforward graphical user interfaces (GUIs) where the whole purpose is to draw pictures or read aloud information from files on your hard disk. These computers will not understand commands that you type into a text editor or even an email application. Other computers are more like your typical old typewriter — they do have a user interface, but it's deficient level and doesn't understand anything other than text. You can ask these computers to type out information, but they will only understand the text you typed in.

So in the case of our iPod example, if you tried to use a GUI-based computer to transfer your songs, it wouldn't be able to tell which songs you wanted to move. And if you tried to say an older computer based on text commands what type of file is stored on your hard drive, it would not figure out how you want it to operate. The critical point here is that code can only go to understand and work on the necessary data.

So, why do you use a computer? Well, as I said before, computers can do many things that we are not capable of doing ourselves. In some ways, programming is like playing chess and designing your pieces and thinking ahead by the end of the game — it is quite a fantastic experience.
What's it like to code? You are writing new code every day! Like most things in life, though, there is a learning curve.

The more you code, the easier it becomes.

You will start to get a sense of what is possible and what works best by trying different things out. So while you may sometimes have a little trouble understanding exactly how things are working, you will find that you begin to understand how computers work much better over time. If this sounds like fun to you, then coding could be the career for you!

Chapter 4.

Popular Programming Languages

The popular programming languages that are in use the most today. They include Java, Python, PHP, C/C++, and Ruby. This book compares these languages and gives insight into the top features of each one. A conclusion is given at the end of this book to help readers decide which language they want to learn. The author also suggests courses that can be used to learn these programming languages online without having to buy any textbooks or other materials to learn it from scratch.

This provides many valuable sources for people interested in learning new skills and getting some helpful information about popular programming languages. The book is very lengthy, but it provides you with a practical guide to decide which programming languages you might want to learn first. Many benefits can be provided by knowing how to program, such as the flexibility of getting a job in programming. You can also earn more money since you will have control over your career and how much you get paid for it.

This part of the book compares Java, Python, PHP, and Ruby in terms of popularity, websites created using that language, and their ability to develop mobile applications on Google

Android or Apple iOS. An exceptionally long list of websites designed using these programming languages allows you to browse through to find many helpful sites.

This part of the book provides a comparison between C and C++. It is based on the quotes from programmers who prefer either one language over the other. It also describes strategies used by companies and institutions to improve their business application using one or both programming languages.

In this part of the book, you will find out how Python can be used for various purposes. First, you will learn in-depth about how Python can be used for web development and which website platforms are supported. The author also provides you with a few different ways to get Python, such as downloading from the Python website itself.

This part of the book samples 5 of the best programming textbooks and provides its readers with details about each of them. You will find abstracts of each textbook which is extremely helpful if you're having trouble deciding which book to buy first. It also gives you helpful tips on finding more books from a local library or through online websites, such as Amazon or eBay.

This part of the book provides an in-depth comparison between PHP and Ruby on Rails. You will find quotes from programmers and bosses of famous companies asked about their experience with these programming languages.

This part of the book features a test of some popular programming languages about their performance. You will find several different tests on Python, Ruby, Java and C#. The author provides a helpful set of instructions that you can follow to perform the test yourself if you have questions about it.

This part of the book compares Java and Android to each other. It is based on the quotes from programmers who prefer either one language over the other. The book also describes strategies used by companies and institutions to improve their business application using one or both of these programming languages

Chapter 5.

Understanding the Structure of a Program

This part of the book aims to get you quickly started on the basics of coding, teaching you the first step:

"Understanding the structure of a program".

The Program Structure

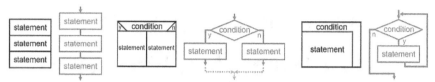

In our example, we have a program that simply prints hello and goodbye. The syntax tells us that we create two different functions with their data and logic for each. It is often referred to as procedural programming because it has separate procedures which can be executed at any time in any order.

Introduction to Programming Variables

As mentioned above, every programming language has its own set of rules and quirks, but they all share one thing in common: variables.

Variable Data Types

The data types define how values are stored within a variable. In our example above, the variables used are integer and string. Each represents specific values or bit sequences of bits. The int represents integers, while the string represents text. In addition to the data type, each variable contains a value of its own and can be changed by the programmer when run through the computer's compiler. As an example:

1 . 23 + 4 .56 = 27.56

When you add 23 and 4.5, you get 27.6, but instead of storing it as 27, we store it in a variable. It would be like having 1 dollar on hand and saying, "I have one dollar," except you'll say "$1" instead of "one dollar." Please note that every programming language has its jargon for variables such as int or string or float and so on.

We will go into more detail when we learn how to manipulate variables in our following tutorial.

Understanding the Structure of a Program: Subroutine Function

Our example above is known as procedural programming because it has separate procedures which can be executed at any time in any order. In this example, we have the primary function, which is executed first. This is the beginning of our program, and in programming jargon, it's known as the primary procedure. The program can call upon a series of subroutines (functions) that will then be executed at any time. Each process has its values and logic that can be used by it or with other functions.

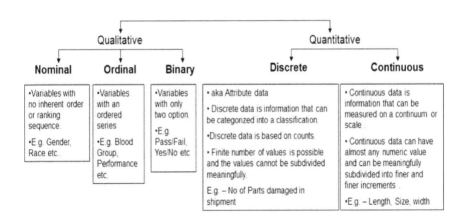

Commands & Logic

We use commands to direct the interpreter (computer) on how to execute our program. Commands are the exact instructions you're telling your program to manage. Some common commands used in programming are print, input, if, else and while.

In addition to instructions, logic is also used. Sense tells the computer to execute a specific command based on certain conditions. For example, the if knowledge allows us to check certain conditions and instruct the interpreter (computer) to perform one or more actions.

Understanding the Structure of a Program: Data Assessor

In our example, we have a main function that can call upon a series of subroutines. These are called data assessors as they answer the question, "what is this variable?" A data assessor is like an entry point to your program that helps you respond this variable. For each variable in your program, there needs to be one and only one data accessor for that variable. If you create two or more variables with their own separate data accessors, your program will not run correctly.

Programming Quirks and Tips

There are a few quirks to keep in mind as you start programming. For example, if you want to create a program that asks the user for their name, don't put the user's name in quotes. This is because every single variable has to start with a letter or an underscore (_). So "Alice" will not work as it will be interpreted as Alice, which is not a valid variable. If you need to ask the user for their name, you should use "username." The underscore character (_) is used to separate different variables from one another, so they are not mixed up. There is also something called scope. This is a fundamental concept that you probably already know. The scope allows our program to know what variables are defined in the program and where they are defined. Their position determines this, so the first variable on any line of code is called the local scope and can be accessed without needing to write out the name of that variable. But if you start to print out variables outside of your subroutines, you will need to write out their names.

Programming Terminology

Classes, Objects, Variables, and Functions.

The object-oriented programming methodology creates a more structured and orderly way to store data within your computer programs. Object-oriented programming is based on what we learn in high school and college, but is used differently in the real world. This methodology creates classes of objects that are designed to be similar to the real world objects.

A class is a way of organizing your program into different groups with similar values, similar methods or actions (functions), and similar properties. Class is derived from a set of values that are known as attributes. The attributes can be anything from numbers to strings or built-in variables such as location, size, speed, time, etc... In our program above, we have one class called main, which has one attribute called EXE. That is, the EXE variable is defined in the program.

By creating a class, we can make objects that inherit this class. For example, in our program, we created a class called "Main," which inherits from the "Main" class. We can then create an object called main using this class (it will be called main).

A variable is like any other variable in your program, except it can be used by many classes/objects and has its scope. Unlike variables that are defined within one subroutine, variables defined outside of subroutines are called global variables. Variables defined in the same class all have the same scope, which means they can be accessed at any time within that class. Variable scope is determined by where the variable is defined (the local scope or global scope), but once a variable (local or global) is defined, it always has a scope.

Chapter 6.

Different Types of Programs

Let's look at the different types of programs and see which ones might be best for each experience level.

Where Should You Learn to Code? Many people don't realize about coding because it can be learned in many different ways.

If you're new to programming, an excellent place to start would be with a language like Python or Java. These languages are easier for beginners because they do not require prior knowledge of any other programming language to get started with them. Once you've mastered these two languages, you'll probably want to try your hand at C++ or PHP (or something else entirely).

If you have already learned one or more programming languages, but are looking for something new to try, then you'll probably want to try a new language that takes different approaches from the ones that you already know. This means that C++ and Java might be a good place to start. These languages are similar enough to others that you can make the transition from them relatively easy (once you know another language).

If you're already an experienced coder, then there's no need to replace your current development environment with something new. However, it can still help if you switch over Js just long enough to get familiar with a different approach.

Once this happens, it will be easier for you to learn other languages in the future.

Knowledge of the Internet: If you're new to programming, you'll want to make sure that you understand how the internet works before you begin your new adventure. Although it might sound overwhelming at first, the internet isn't that hard to understand.
It might not be necessary for you to learn HTML and CSS before you start learning web development (they're pretty simple languages, after all), but it will help if you do.

Learn About the Internet:

Don't Wait To Learn To Code: The best time to learn is now. It doesn't matter if you're 100 years old or ten years old, or even somewhere in-between. There are no limits on who can learn how things work. If you know how to read, you can learn how things work. If you are ready to start learning programming languages, or if you have already started, then it's time for you to get yourself one of the above books and begin your journey into the world of coding.

This doesn't mean that everything will be easy going from here on in.

There are always new challenges ahead, but if learning to code interests you, then the journey will be worth it. The best way for things to become more accessible is for more people to learn how things work. The more people that know how to code, the easier it will be for you to learn. So, what are you waiting for?

Chapter 7.

How Is a Program Built?

There are several different approaches to building a program, but in this beginner's guide, we will focus on one strategy: top-down design.

Top-down design is a method of programming where the highest-level modules are designed first and then the lower-level modules are designed based on these high-level modules. This approach works great for beginners as they can easily break their program down into logical pieces.

Step One: Planning Out Your Program

Before you get started, it's crucial to have an idea of what your program should do. You might want to think about things like the input and output for your programs and what data it will process. Once you believe you have a good idea, it's time to get started!

Step Two: Creating a Data Structure for Your Program

The first thing we'll do is create our data structure. In this case, we're going to use an array. We will store three numbers within this array: a list of integers and two floating-point numbers. These will represent some user input that we'll process within our program later on.

Step Three: Building the Main Program Loop

Now that we have a place to store the data and know what our program needs to do, it's time to build the main program loop (also known as the main function).

Step Four: Building the Processors

The processors are a series of functions that will run in sequence. These processors receive the data and do something with it, like adding numbers, taking away numbers, or converting bytes to integers.
Step Five: Building the Final Program Loop Now that we've seen what the processors should do, we can build our final program loop (also known as the main function). When you're finished writing this program, you will have a C++ program looking like this:

```
#include <stdio.h>
int main()
```

Step Six: Creating a Data Structure

Now that we have the main program loop, we need to create our data structure. Since we kept track of our data from the previous step, this is easy to do:

int main()

Step Seven: Building the Processors

Now that we have created our data structure, it's time to start building the processors. The first processor should receive some input from the user and convert it to an integer to be added to the list of integers. To get started, you will want to write your first processor function. This will be called convert to integer().

Since you'll be receiving input from the user, you will want to have an if statement to verify that the information is a number.

Step Eight: Building the Final Program Loop

Now that we have our convert_to_integer() processor function created, we can add it to the main program loop.
Now that you've added convert_to_integer() to your main program loop, it's time to build your next processor function. This will be called add_numbers().
Inside your new add_numbers() processor function, you'll need another if statement (or else statement) since you should only add numbers and not convert an integer to a floating-point number.

Step Nine: Building the Final Program Loop

Now that you have your add_numbers() processor function created, you can add it to your main program loop.
The final processor will be called display_numbers(). This program will output the number list and the sum so let's get started!
You will want to check that the user has entered at least two numbers because they won't be able to add anything together if they didn't.

Step Ten: Creating a Data Structure

Now that we have our final program loop complete, let's create a data structure. This will store our list of numbers and our sum so we can output them later on.

Save your program and compile it. If there are no errors, you should be ready to run your finished program!
The first thing the user will want to do is enter some data to make sure they can. When the user runs our program, they will see our prompt asking for some data. Once they enter a number, we will write it to an array and then ask the user for another number. This process will repeat until the user enters zero numbers or a negative number.

Step Eleven: Building the Final Program Loop

Now that we have confirmed that the user entered numbers, we're ready to build our final program loop (also known as main function).

After the user enters data into our processor, we will assign that data to our list of integers and then we will add all those numbers together.

Finally, let's output the array of numbers and the sum to make sure everything worked as expected.

Appendix C: Easy C++ Programming Tips

Coding is fun but it can be frustrating too. While you might be tempted to throw your hands up and go back to the drawing board, there are a few things you can do to help with those programming headaches. We saved the best for last, so let's get to reviewing!

Coding Tips Are Your Best Friend

It doesn't matter if your program works. If it's impossible that anyone would ever use it, then it's not a great program. Think of all the times people have been let down by programs they believed would help them but ended up being useless.

Chapter 8.

How Is a Program Executed?

The first thing with any program is translating it from the original programming language (usually in something like C++ or Java) into machine code (zeros and ones). This is done by a program called the compiler.

A program always starts with what is called "statements" or "instructions," which tell the computer what to do, either sequentially or in parallel (i.e., by doing them at the same time). For example, if you want the program to print out "Hello" followed by "World," you would give it the instruction:
print("Hello") print("World")

In machine code, this is written as:

0x420000 Hello 0x420001 World 0x420002

Where "0x" represents a hexadecimal number (the kind used in computers to describe numbers). This shows how each line of code is broken up into its instructions. Each instruction looks like a single letter of the alphabet so that the computer will know what to do with it. (This is called "coding.")

BASIC (which stands for "Beginner's All-purpose Symbolic Instruction Code") was designed to be as easy as possible to

---

learn for people who have never programmed before. It uses only a few characters that can be typed using a standard keyboard to write each line of code. BASIC has been around since the late 1950s and is still in use today by programming hobbyists and in many schools, where it is used to introduce programming languages in general. You don't need any special equipment or software to learn about or try out programs written using BASIC.

The most straightforward BASIC programs are written using a few keywords which come from the original version of the language, back in the 1960s; they are:

PRINT : Prints a line of text on the screen STORE : Stores a number into a variable (a name for an area of memory) READ : Reads a line of text from the keyboard INTO : Stores or prints out one value that comes from several numbers and/or variables. LOOP : Repeats the next line of code until something true is no longer valid. GOTO: Jumps to another part of code (instrumental when writing programs) END: Ends program.

These keywords are used in combination to make a complete program. For example, the program below prints out the text, "Hello World" on the screen, followed by a number between 0 and 10:

10 PRINT "Hello World" 20 INPUT n 30 IF n<0 THEN GOTO 80 40 PRINT n 50 GOTO 30 80 END

The first line tells the computer to start reading instruction from the beginning of the following line. The computer, therefore, processes the second line (#10). Notice that the number is prefixed with an apostrophe once again, as in the earlier "Hello World" program. This is so that the computer knows to read the line as a number.

The third line (#20) tells the computer what to do if it finds something called a "conditional" statement, which is used to make sure that something is true before carrying on with whatever comes after it. In this case, it checks whether or not the user has pressed a key on their keyboard. If they have pressed a key, whatever comes between brackets (the lines below) will be processed by the computer. If not, then the computer will carry on with the rest of line #20.

The fourth line (#30) checks if the number that comes after is less than zero (i.e., it has a "negative sign"). If so, it jumps back to line #80. This is where everything will be repeated as long as that number is negative.

Therefore, the fourth line (#30) tells the computer that whatever it can see before this point in the program should be repeated until it sees a bar called "End." If you wanted the computer to carry on until it saw a "Stop" or "End," which might be used for debugging, then you would write this:
30 IF n<0 THEN GOTO 80 40 PRINT n 50 GOTO 30 80 END.

This is called a program that "loops." It means that whatever happens happened again and again. If everything was printed out when you step through this loop (by pressing the "Enter" key), it looks like this:
As can be seen from these examples, there are several ways to write BASIC programs. For example, there are two different ways of writing the line (#30), which checks if the number is less than zero.

30 IF n<0 THEN GOTO 80

This is one way, which uses a single line "IF" statement. The other way, which uses two lines to write the same statement, looks like this:

30 IF n<0THEN GOTO 80

The computer is programmed to read the line by starting at the beginning of each line of code and looking at it row by row. This means that when it finds the "THEN," it will stop reading that line and carry on with whatever follows after. This is why the two ways of writing this statement are called different programming languages: BASIC or Visual Basic.

PRINT "Hello World" PRINT "Hello world" PRINT "Hello, World" END
A question that was asked earlier about programs such as this was why we needed to put line numbers after the first line. As you've seen, the program is written to read each line of code from left to right. The computer can therefore read the lines in any order it wants. Often programmers find it more convenient to use line numbers to know exactly where they are in the overall program.

Textboxes

Most Visual Basic programs will contain many lines of code. Sometimes you want to refer to a particular line, or you might mean something in particular within the program. For example, you might want to refer back to a specific part of the program, or you might want to display a list of some sort. Textboxes are one way of doing this. They allow you to write text as if it was part of your code and be able to access it later on by using the commands such as "PRINT", "PRINTA" and so on, which were described above.

Chapter 9.

What Are Program Statements?

Program statements are the individual instructions that you, as the programmer, give to your computer.

Code is often written in a programming language. A programming language is a set of symbols and rules used to create commands for computers to execute. Each line of code in a program statement needs to be spaced out with one space between each word and wrapped at 80 characters so the code can be easily read by humans and machines alike.

We all know how frustrating it can be when you want something done but don't know how or where to start. I'll take you from the beginning, explaining everything you need to know to create your programs. I'll show you how to write, compile and run a program. Each section will give you another skill, which will build on the previous skills and knowledge and give you an ever-increasing understanding of programming.

I want to make programming easy for beginners just like me! You see, I started my first programming course at university with absolutely no prior experience in coding whatsoever. I had no idea what the lecturer was talking about or how he expected us to do our coursework. This frustration led me on a mission to find out how others had been taught programming or how they had learned themselves, and what difficulties they had come across. I found out that many people started learning by themselves as well, but they quickly became defeated and stumbled across a difficult hurdle. This hurdle is what I'm here to help you get over.

So let's get coding!

What is a Program?

A computer program is simply a list of instructions for the computer to follow, just like any other list. You can have shopping lists, day-to-day tasks, or even schoolwork - it all has the same common feature; they're all lists of things to do. These instructions are called "statements," and each statement in your program will help tell the computer how to accomplish your task.

Some statements are simple, such as writing one letter to the screen, whereas other statements are more complex and include lots of things, all happening simultaneously!

Our main program will be called 'Program.BAS,' so it needs a unique name. It must also be saved in its folder called 'Videos,' and the file extension must be '.BAS.' Without this, you won't be able to run your program.

All of these factors need to match, or else your program can't run correctly or at all. So if you're having problems with this section, please make sure that you've followed everything 100%.

This is what our folder structure should look like:

Codey v1.0 is a Windows application. This means that the program can only be run on Windows computers, and you need to have the appropriate software to run your program. Linux users may think they don't need to follow these rules, but this is a Windows-only tutorial, so please follow!

Important Note: If you're on Mac, then the app probably won't work properly. There are many programs out there that are incompatible with Mac OS X.

Many things go into making a computer program which we like to call "coding. Coding isn't just what you're doing right now. It's the act of taking a program from your head and turning it into something the computer can understand.

All of this coding will be done using a programming language such as Python, C#, C++ or Basic - there are thousands of different languages and they all have their features.

Our program will be coded in Microsoft's BASIC programming language, which is relatively simple to learn, and is an easy way to begin coding if you have no experience of what it involves.

If you already know how to code another language, this tutorial probably won't help you teach you anything new.

Program Statements

```
Output - JavaApplication35 (run)  ✕

run:
Please enter a word: hello
Please enter the first letter: h
Please enter the second letter: e
Please enter the third letter: l
Please enter the fourth letter: o
Please enter the fifth letter: p
You lose!
BUILD SUCCESSFUL (total time: 11 seconds)
```

When you write a program, you're writing individual commands for the computer to follow. You'll be writing these lines of code one at a time. A program statement is the same as a sentence in speech. If the speaker were writing this on their phone, then they would write it down as "I will go to the store and buy some bread."

Statements can often contain several instructions all at once. These instructions are run in order, so if we wanted to tell our computer to "Buy some bread," then we'd write that statement like this:

I want you all to note how many spaces are separating each instruction and how many characters are in each education. Also, take note of how that statement is wrapped onto a new line, and the instruction is 80 characters long. If you're using any other program to write your code, then this may not apply to you - just write your code so humans easily read it and so the computer can run it properly.

Now that we know what a program statement is, let's look at how our BASIC programming language works.

Syntax tells the computer exactly how we want our program to be written, what syntax we should use and where/how everything should be spaced out. It also tells us where each instruction begins and ends.

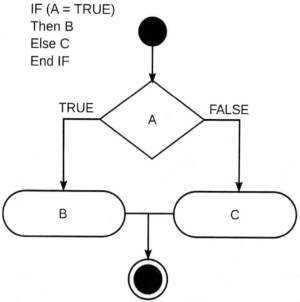

```
IF (A = TRUE)
Then B
Else C
End IF
```

Program statements are just programs on their own. They may tell the computer to run other statements in our program or say to the computer to do something. Each instruction will say to the computer to do something specific, just like how a sentence has different words for different situations.

All of our program's commands will be written between these brackets, { } .

Brackets simply contain everything for our program, so anything written within them will be read by the computer and acted upon.

Statements - what should go here?

So what goes in between the brackets? Every line of code can contain one or more statements, and each statement runs independently from every other. If you remove one of your statements, then the program will still run without any problems.

Without your program statements, you can't run any of your programs.

Programming languages allow you to format your code however you like as long as you follow the rules. If you want to add more instructions or some conditional statement then add more code between those brackets! The computer will ignore it, though, so don't worry about it too much - go ahead and write that "IF...

Chapter 10.

Data Types, Variables and Operators

Data Types: Variables and Operators are two of the three fundamental pieces of programming that help you understand how to code. This book will cover data types, variables, and operators with a focus on the basics. Variables are containers for storing data (such as numbers), while Operators are for performing actions on the data in those containers. Data types help you manage your program's memory usage by telling it what sort of things it can store.

Variables:

A variable is a container for storing information in your program (such as numbers). The computer stores all kinds of information about your program and its environment in memory, like warehouses or storage areas. When your program needs to use that information, it asks the computer for it.

Operators: An operator is a symbol used in programming to change how a value is used in your program. For example, = means that you are assigning a number to an existing variable. The equals sign can also be used as an assignment operator. 15 = 15 tells the computer that when you say 15, assign it to the variable named 15.

The Key Concepts: We now need to discuss what variables are for and how they work their magic. The computer will use a certain amount of memory for your program and left to its own devices, it will keep using that memory until you tell it to stop. When that happens, your program won't work correctly. The computer won't store all of the information about what you are doing in the program. So how do you tell the computer when you need a new piece of memory?

The Basic Rule: First, create variables (or place data in variables) and then use them in your programs! This is going to sound slightly contradictory. However, this means that you write code to handle all of the information in your program and when it needs to find a new piece of memory for your program, you tell it where to find that recent memory. For this process to work, you need to understand about data types. Data Types: When you create a variable, you tell the computer how much memory is needed and what kind of data it can store. This tells the computer that if the variable contains some kind of information, it will know precisely how to access it and display it on your screen (or do other things). Without this information, the computer cannot understand what you want it to do and will be forced to shut down.

Data Types are Like: let's say you are running a clothing store. Since you sell clothes, you decide to use an inventory system that counts how many different items of clothing you have in stock. You can visualize your inventory system as a large shelf with many other boxes all over the place filled with clothes. If your program needs some clothes, it can go over to the shelf, grab a box and take it back to the dressing room for someone to try on. These boxes are like variables because they store information about lists of things in the world (like your stock of clothes).

Data Types are Not Like: There is a big difference between these variables boxes and the sheets of paper used to keep inventory. These boxes also have places on each of them to label what they contain. However, there is no way to know what the box contains without opening it and checking for yourself. If you want the computer to know that box 1 contains dresses, then your program will need to open that box, look at the label added by you, and figure out what became your clothes when you opened the box.

To tell the computer about a variable's data type, put a + sign in front of it (these signs are called prefixes because they come before other signs or symbols). Your inventory system should have a label on each box that tells you what is inside of it. The computer will see the + sign and use it to figure out what type of clothes you have in each box (this process is called data typing). In programming, the boxes are variables. Adding a prefix makes the variable data typed, meaning that the computer knows how to use that variable.

Here's an example: You are using a variable named bob and you want the computer to know that this variable contains employees in your program. Then you would type bob+, which means employee. You can create as many variables as you want by changing the bob+ with another word such as clerk+ or cashier+. Since you have done this, the computer knows that bob is an employee. It has no idea what it is holding at this point, just that bob contains individual employees and that it can display these employees in your program the same way it displays clothing or any other kind of inventory.

Another way to tell a variable what kind of information it can hold is to use a - sign in front of the variable's name. This will tell the computer that the variable can store any information (called general). Let's say you are a teacher and have many grades to give in your program. You can create a variable named grades+ which will allow your program to take any kind of grade, print it out on the screen and then add an appropriate + sign in front of it. This is how the computer takes an ordinary letter grade, such as B+.

There are also special symbols called prefixes that come before other signs or symbols. While these don't tell the computer what kind of information is being stored in the variables (at least not directly), they say to the computer what it can do with it.

Chapter 11.

The Importance of Strings

When it comes to writing programs that communicate with one another, there are many different types of computer programming languages. Some programming languages use keywords and numbers, others use symbols and a combination of both, and then there are those that happily take up the majority of their space with strings.

The string type is useful because it can be used to represent any kind of detailed element in any graphical interface. For example, the command "Move ten meters East" written in Python would look something like this: "move('10m','E')". As you know, the Python text editor is straightforward. The only thing it needs to figure out is how to move something.

If you were writing a program that could be used to manipulate some part of the user interface, you would probably not want to use numbers. You would want some way to tell your program what buttons should be pressed or what coordinates a mouse's movement should correspond to. And in order for a command string like "Move ten meters East" or anything else to do anything useful, the information it contained must be stored somewhere and associated with some other kind of entity.

This is where strings are so helpful: They can store any amount of information that can be transmitted between two applications. Our "Move ten meters East" command would be represented as:

move('10m','E')

Now, if a program like the Python editor were to ask for a list of coordinates or button commands, all it would need to do is create a string with each element in the list. This way, when you are reading an element from the string you can treat it exactly like any other entry in an array.

When it comes to using strings for commands and data, having just one kind of information stored in them can be very limiting; especially if you plan on sending strings thousands or millions of miles between devices. This is where the idea of "encoding" comes in.

Encoding is the process of changing a string's content into something that a computer can use more efficiently for sending and storage. To understand how encoding works, you need to look at this simple example.

Let's say that there is an application which has been programmed to send a command to all of the devices in

Earth's environment: "Save all data." The application which sends this command would look something like this:

```
here(s = 'Save all data.') >>> s.encode('UTF8') >>> print(s)
Save+all+data.
```

One of the important things to understand about encoding is that it happens in both directions. Before an encoded string can be sent anywhere, it needs to be decoded. In other words, in order for our application above to be able to execute the command "Save all data.", it needs to know how to receive and decode a string like we've made here:

save'all'data .

The second important thing you need to understand is that encodings have names; and the name of the encoding we used above is UTF-8. An encoding is exactly like a programming language; it has a name, an interpreter and it can be used to communicate with foreign entities.
Now that you've learned how encodings work and how strings are used to represent commands, we can talk about how we can interpret the command "Save all data." in Python using just a string.

Translation: Take our string "Save all data." and convert it into an ASCII string, then decode the string so it can be used as a command. We need first to convert the string into an ASCII format because Python 3 uses the ascii encoding which converts strings to uppercase letters. Remember that strings can contain any amount of pieces of text, so we need to make sure that our command is only going to contain letters or digits in order for it to be understood correctly. Once we have the ASCII string, we need to decode it to an actual command.

To make sure our strings can easily be converted and decoded, we will always use a "private" string referring to the encoding. Let's look at that code again:

```
here(s = 'Save all data.') >>> s.encode('UTF8') >>> print(s)
Save+all+data. >>> s.decode() Save all data.
```

If we go over this code step by step, you'll see that the first time it runs it converts a Python string into an ascii string then it decodes the ascii string into a Python object called a 'string'. Then it can be used like any other command.

The next time around, we can just use the string object's "encode" method to convert the string into a Python string that is UTF-8 for saving all data. Also, remember that strings also have methods that can be used for converting between multiple different encodings in addition to the convert between ASCII and UTF-8 that we used in this exercise. Let's look at another example:

```
here(s = 'ananas') >>> s.encode('UTF8') >>> print(s) ananas
>>> s.decode() ananas >>> s.encode('ASCII') ananas
```

The last thing you need to know about encoding is that Python uses a number of encodings as defined by the variable "encoding". These encodings are:

ascii = 'ASCII'

iso_8859_1 = 'latin1'

utf_8 = 'utf-8'

Now that you know everything you need to know about encoding, let's talk about how we can use this knowledge to

make our own program more efficient when sending and receiving strings.
Let's take a look at the following data:

```
data = ['test','joke','name']

print('All',data,'of',len(data),'with',len(data),'no',len(data),'new lines.')
```

The code above gets the length of a list and outputs it in multiple ways. So why is this a big deal? Well, if we were to add one new item to our list, how many lines of output would we get? Let's find out. Here's what we'll do: add one new item to our list, then run the code above. Here's the code:

```
data = ['test','joke','name','newline']

print('All',data,'of',len(data),'with',len(data),'no',len(data),'new lines.')
```

We get the following output: All 4 of 5 with 0 newlines. . If you're observant, you might have noticed that we got one more line than before. This is because the list was empty and so when it printed len(data) , it added a newline because newlines aren't allowed in Python, but they are allowed in some programming languages such as C++.

Chapter 12.

Iterative Programming

Iterative programming is a powerful technique for transitioning from vague, undefined systems to more specific and refined ones through repeated development cycles. The process typically begins with an initial set of requirements that is then implemented quickly and imperfectly. The system is then evaluated and improved based on the initial goal to meet or exceed this target.

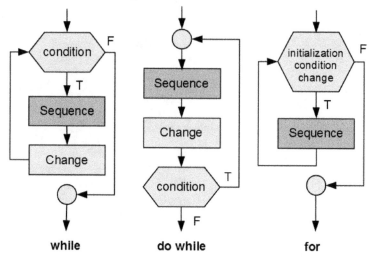

The process repeats until the system approaches perfection regarding its original specifications – at which point maintenance takes over to keep things running smoothly. This style of development initiates a cycle called the "iteration," which starts again after completion with a new set of requirements or objectives (hence "iterative"). It is well suited for software systems in which conditions are constantly changing or added as a product matures.

There are several iterations within the iteration (i.e., a hierarchy of iterations) that add detail to the system in a step-by-step fashion.

Building an iterative approach into an organization's development cycle typically requires planning upfront so that time can be set aside throughout the project to implement and evaluate each iteration; allowing flexibility for changes; defining what constitutes successful completion of an iteration as well as project completion, so that there are consistent goals at all levels; and providing structure in the form of a framework to communicate what the system does and doesn't do.

Iterative methods are generally designed to help a team develop a solution incrementally, in small portions, and interactively. This is opposed to waterfall methodologies that impose an entire solution in one go from the very beginning.

The focus of iterative methodologies is on being "continuously improving" rather than "frequently shipped"; thus, the term iterative here does not necessarily refer to the cyclical nature of the methodological approach but rather about continuous improvement. In this sense, the adjective "iterative" means that systems are built as small modules that can be incrementally evaluated and improved. It is an incremental approach to delivering solutions that enables modular implementation.

The iterative approach is a common practice in product design and development, particularly in the computer industry. It is also relevant to project management and other areas. By applying the framework of an iteration to project management, projects can be planned with a short-term goal (or milestone). Each major phase or iteration of the project then adds some critical functionality that users need in order for the system to be useful. The iterative approach in project management enables problems and issues to be spotted early on and allows planning for time contingencies. This is crucial because it helps ensure that deliverables from each iteration are actually practical and usable by end-users.

The iterative approach also works well in a project environment with changing requirements. Project managers can plan on using the iterative approach when they expect the end-user to dictate system functionality. Plus, by baselining requirements at the beginning of each iteration, project managers can control how features get implemented and ensure that they are coordinated with other features planned for future iterations.

The key to an effective iterative development process is identifying potential issues early, allowing time and budget for corrective action so that delivery dates are not jeopardized. This is also important because it helps make sure that deliverables from each iteration are actually practical and usable by end-users.

For example, a project manager should consider the following issues when planning an iteration:

This helps ensure that deliverables from each iteration are valuable and usable by end-users. For example, if the requirements for a new feature change at the last moment, the team can work to accommodate changes and still meet the budget/schedule. This is vital because it helps ensure that deliverables from each iteration are practical and usable by end-users.

The iterative approach to development also works well in a project environment with changing requirements. Project managers can plan on using the iterative approach when they expect the end-user to dictate system functionality. Plus, by baselining requirements at the beginning of each iteration, project managers can control how features get implemented and ensure that they are coordinated with other features planned for future iterations.

The key to an effective iterative development process is to identify potential issues early, allowing time and budget for corrective action so that delivery dates are not jeopardized. This helps ensure that deliverables from each iteration are valuable and usable by end-users.

Software re-engineering is another technique for transitioning from vague, undefined systems to more specific and refined ones through repeated development cycles. The process typically begins with an initial set of requirements that is then implemented quickly and imperfectly. The system is then evaluated and improved based on the initial goal to meet or exceed this target.

In software engineering, a "specification" or "requirements document" is a standard document communicated to project stakeholders or "users" during the planning and for construction in order to ensure that the system conforms to some defined set of expectations. It prescribes goals and objectives, specifies a scope of functionality, creates possibilities for design decisions, adds constraints upon functionality, and defines relationships with other systems for interaction purposes.

Re-engineering is the process of transforming, improving or redesigning a software system, based on analysis and feedback that reveals opportunities to improve functionality, efficiency or quality or to respond to changes in the marketplace. In specific terms, it is used concerning software projects.

Early rethinking of requirements (prioritizing), scope and architecture through rapid prototyping.

Using a spiral development process where specification documents are used as input for requirements engineering.

They are integrating design with testing, using test-driven development (TDD) as part of the improvement cycle, deploying on an early production system.

One of the more difficult re-engineering parts involves decommissioning legacy systems, typically not many years old, and replacing them with new or upgraded systems. As the project looks to replace the old system, it should be determined what will be the benefit gained from each decision made and then addressed accordingly.

Chapter 13.

Logical Grouping of Code

Java is a language that has curly braces, semicolons, and a variety of keywords. It is broken down into logical groupings of code.

A "logical grouping of code" is a phrase used to describe an independent section of computer instructions in Java (which are usually surrounded by curly braces). The following statements would be valid examples:

```
int x = 1;
int y = 0;
int z = y * x.
```

The statements here are being used to show how there can be multiple lines in a single logical grouping. These particular examples do not do anything more than just set the values for variables (x,y, and z).

Ideally, these lines of code should be placed together because they are related to the same problem. Consider if we changed x to two and then y to 9:

```
int x = 2;
int y = 9;
int z = y * x.
```

There is the logic being applied here. The variable z will be equal to 18, instead of randomly assigning values for x and y (such as a=3 and b=9); there is a connection between them. This makes maintaining code much easier in the future when someone else must come along and try to make sense out of what you did.

The only thing holding you back when writing code is the fact that you can't read it yourself. Don't be discouraged just because it seems too complex or too big to understand at first. Just keep going at it, learn by doing, and you'll get the hang of it!

It is important to know those good programmers do not write a lot of code during a project. They are much more focused on the overall design of their program in order to get a general idea about what they are working on before they write the lines of code for it.

A good programmer is willing to take a second and consider the simplicity of what they are trying to do, the possibilities, and if there are much better ways of going about doing things. This results in better developed code and a lot more flexibility when it comes to making changes.

Code should be developed in smaller segments that focus on lots of different areas. Smaller segments allow for more flexible coding, which can be used as a base for future projects and can make updates easier to do later down the line. These segments should not become cumbersome, as that would defeat the purpose of creating them in the first place.

When you are beginning a new program, you must understand the fundamental basics in order to build off of them later on. If you keep trying to solve everything simultaneously, you'll end up in an endless loop and not getting anywhere. Start by setting some initial parameters for the program that can be used as a starting point (or a base) for your code.

For example, let's say we want to write a program that will control our car's radio based on its speed. We should be able to define a variable that we can use to control the speed of our radio and have it output that data back into the program on the computer screen.

"Let's see how things go" is a phrase heard very often in programming. Rather than getting frustrated with something, take your time and see if you can figure out what you need to do or solve the problem when you are presented with it. Code is meant to be worked with, and you should not feel like you need to do everything perfectly from the beginning.
It is better to take your time trying to solve a problem than just rushing through it. However, there are cases where we need the computer to wait in order for us to accomplish something:

System.out.println("I'm Waiting"); // Do something.

This will cause the program that is currently running on our computer screen to pause its normal execution and wait for us to tell it what we want it to do next.
Here's an example of how this could be used : while (x != 0) { //do something x = x / 2; } // System.out.println("I'm done");

During the above program, x equals 2, so we will go through and divide it by 2 each time through the loop (the while). This will then give us a value of 1 for y, which is then put into a variable called z. You can then use z to control the frequency on your radio's display.

Please see: Java for Absolute Beginners - Coding for Absolute Beginners
A program consists of three parts: input, transformation, and output (or simply just "input", "output", and "output"). These three steps must be completed in order to compile a program written in Java successfully. This means that in order to make the program work, you need to follow these steps:

-1. The first step is input. This means that the program needs data from the user, which is usually entered by telling the computer what you want to be done and how you want it done. If you have a variable called "x", then it would be entered as something like this:

int x = 1.

This way, the computer knows that it should interpret this as an integer (i.e.: a whole number) value (1). The values that we put into data-driven programs are known as inputs.

-2. The second step is transformation. This means that the program must take the variable and do something with it. This is a much more complicated step, but what it really means is that we need to show our users how things are changing based on the input they give us (or, in other words, offering them information). If you had a variable called "myAge" and you wanted to write your name based on its value, then you could do this by doing something like this:

System.out.println("Hello myAge")

This would change what was output by the program every time myAge changed (i.e. every time the user changed their age). The values that we put into programs are known as outputs.

-3. The third and last step is output. This means that the program needs to save or print out the data it has worked with so that it can be stored somewhere else (usually on a hard drive, memory stick, etc.). This step is pretty easy because all you have to do is use something like this:

System.out.println("Hello myAge")

In order to save what was done in our program (i.e. print out "hello myAge") onto a separate file, you could use something like this:

System.out.println("Hello myAge").

Chapter 14.

What Is Object-Oriented Programming?

Object-Oriented Programming (OOP) is a programming paradigm that makes use of objects and their interactions. Objects are data structures containing both the data and functions that operate on it, which contrasts with pure procedural programming.

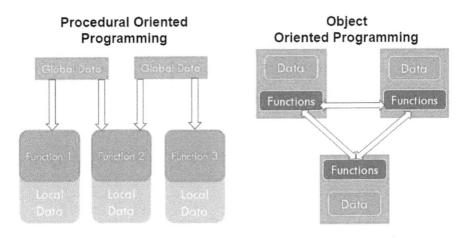

What Does Object-Oriented Programming Mean?

Object-oriented programming is the technique of breaking down complex algorithms into more straightforward, more manageable parts to simplify development. The complexity of OOP comes from the relationship between these objects and how they interact with each other, instead of how they process information internally.

What Does Object Oriented Programming Not Mean?

In contrast with OOP, is an often misunderstood approach to programming that advocates the programming of every object as if it was a real object when it isn't. OOP is a term that refers to the type of programming used in object-oriented applications. It does not refer to the language or the methodology - each language and design technique can be used independently of others - only how objects are treated. An object-oriented program may use any language as long as it supports data abstraction and inheritance concepts. However, in addition to these fundamental purposes, OOP also provides several advantages over traditional approaches to building software.

What Are the Advantages of Object-Oriented Programming?

OOP has several distinct advantages, including:

1. OOP Encourages Modular Development. The whole idea behind OOP is to break down programs into smaller, more manageable parts. This allows each component to be implemented in minimum time and with easy maintenance after that. The relationship between these parts is designed so that rather than having objects inherit from a base class, each object is easily identifiable with a single function - e.g.

Class.new() called on the class name - which is invoked by passing in one or more parameters - e.g. "objectId".<functionName>().

2. Object-oriented interfaces reveal unnecessary complexity. OOP has the advantage of showing unnecessary complexity in an object-oriented system based on inheritance and polymorphic behavior. For example, when a programmer creates a new object in C++, the programmer must either define all of the internal functions or leave them undefined. If he leaves them undefined, they will most likely create bugs in the program; however, he is duplicating functionality if he defines them all, there is no way for that newly created object to communicate appropriately with other objects.

3. Transparency of data helps avoid bugs. Transparency of data also helps in avoiding bugs. For example, in an object-oriented program, if a programmer is checking whether a variable is less than five, it is easier to say if (x < 5) than if (x <= 5). This is because the first expression shows the intention of the programmer clearly. The second expression requires the reader to infer what it really means.

4. OOP Encourages Code Reuse. OOP allows objects to be combined and inherited from other objects, which increases code reuse. In procedural programming, the programmer must write the program twice, once for each case. Also, with OOP, the programmer can use a library of previously written code and then only have to rewrite a small section to interface with his own code.

5. OOP is easy to update. With procedural programming, any change in the code will also require changes for all functions calling that code. In OOP, if a function or method is changed or added then only that function or procedure needs to be changed.

---

6. Modularity and easy-to-understand modular decomposition make OOP easy to learn and use. With OOP, the programmer is encouraged to think of objects and their relationships and functions as modular sets of reusable parts.

7. OOP Encourages Good Code Design. OOP encourages good coding practice by providing structures that encourage good programming practice. For example, there are separating (sealed) classes for representing data and operations on that data in C++, and in Java, there is a corresponding package for the same purpose.

8. Modularity reduces the chance of errors caused by a single error. Because OOP allows modularization, if an error occurs in one module, it will not affect other modules because each module has its own different interface to other modules so each module can work independently of the others.

9. OOP is easier to debug and maintain. This is because the programmer's code will have fewer functions which can cause bugs. Also, because each class has a different interface to other classes, there is less chance that two classes will be connected to each other improperly.

10. Objects are more easily manipulated and designed in a modular way than procedural objects of the same type. In OOP, an object is more easily manipulated and designed in a modular way than procedural objects of the same type - e.g object creation or destruction.

11. Encapsulation of data makes an assignment of variables easier and therefore reduces the chance for errors caused by insufficient input.

12. Encapsulation of functions to data makes reuse more feasible, thus reducing the chance for errors caused by re-inventing the wheel.

13. Object-oriented languages are easier to learn and thus provide a more intuitive interface to the user than other languages do. OOP's ease of learning is demonstrated with teaching methodology such as object-oriented programming courses in universities.

14. Encapsulation of code makes it easier to insert a component into an existing system. If the function is encapsulated into one or more objects, then changes to that function are isolated from other functions in the program. Also, if the function is encapsulated into one or more objects, then it can be inserted into another program by simply copying the object into place.

15. Encapsulation of data encourages program modularity gives programmers a way to design programs that can easily adapt to change.
16. Object-oriented programming languages' expressive capability provides programmers with a precise and economical way of expressing their intentions in small amounts of code.

17. Encapsulation of data encourages data hiding which helps to eliminate many security problems.

18. Encapsulation encourages the programmer to think about code as self-contained modules that are easier to debug and maintain than code open to outside interference.
19. Encapsulation reduces the complexity of a program. It makes it easier for the programmer to find bugs and fix them because there is less chance that another part of a program

will affect the function being changed (because the function is encapsulated into an object).

Chapter 15.

What Are Client-Server Applications?

In a nutshell, client-server applications are computer software that has a local component and a remote component. The local component is the client (such as your web browser) and the remote component is the server (the software you're using). The data is transmitted from one to the other. When someone wants to log in to an online application, they type in their username and password on their local machine, requesting access from the remote server. The beauty of these applications is that they have a thin boundary between what your computer can do and what happens on a remote machine. This means that with only some basic coding knowledge, you can create games or other high-quality software.

The Turnip

For example, a turnip is a small object that can be used to represent a username, password, or any other kind of encryption on the client. With this simple coding trick, we can make our lives much easier:

In this example: A=A turnip B=B turnip C=C sprouts D=D turns into E=E turnips F=F turns into G=G lettuce. We do not need to use encryption every time we communicate with the server; just use this trick.

Coding Basics

Different languages implement features in different ways. C is one of those languages that have additional features than Java or Python. You aren't allowed to ignore these differences because it will prevent the code from running correctly. To start, we need to learn about all of these differences and how they should be used.

In short, you have four basic types of statements: if statements, for loops, while loops, and switch blocks.

The if Statement

This statement allows you to check whether a specific condition is true or false before executing a particular block of action. In our turnip example code above, we use this statement several times in order to check whether 1 turnip sprouts 2 sprouts 3 turns into 4 lettuce or any other number between 0 and 5.

When a statement finishes executing, the default action is to move the variable up one position, but you can manually move it in the if statement.

For loops, allow us to go through integers or any other list of objects. They're handy for writing simple repetitive code. For example, if we wanted to print out all of the turns of our turnip, we could write it like this:

In our turnip example, we will have a basket containing lettuce seeds, sprouts (1 - 3), lettuce (4 - 5), sprouts (6 - 9), and so on. We will print the number in the square brackets every time through the loop.

The while loop checks whether a particular condition is true or false before checking a block of code and executing it. The code inside the curly brackets is executed at least once, but its execution stops when a particular condition is true. If we wanted to choose one thing from our basket randomly, we could use this while loop.

The code inside the curly brackets will be executed at least once. However, it won't run again until we assign something to turnip Sprouts in line 5.

The switch Statement

This statement allows you to check whether a certain condition is true or false and jump to a certain block of code based on the value. Here's how we could simulate this in our turnip-sprouting example, using different numbers to represent the number of sprouts, starting with 1:
When we say that the "statements inside the curly brackets are executed at least once", it means that they will be executed exactly once. However, if we don't assign anything to turnip Sprouts, it will execute all of these statements just once! We can instruct the switch statement by placing case statements above each part of the code. In our example, we can write the following case statements:

case 1: A= 1; B= 2; C=4; D= 1; E= 2; F= 3; G= 5.
case 2: A = 2; B = 3; C = 4; D = 5.

Case Statement Options

You have a few options when writing your case statements. You can say if or not you want the statement to be executed. You can check to see if there's an exception on either side of the statement. You can also add a default statement if no case statement matches it.

Here's what our code would look like with the correct syntax in place:

In this case, not only will it check A to see if it's 1, 2, 3, or 4...but it will also check B to see if C is between 1 and 5. If neither of those conditions is true, then the default statement at the end will run.

The main idea behind using these three statements in a row is that the while statement controls which code block gets executed and when the for loop returns a new value for an iteration.

The general structure of a C program is to include the header files, declare the variables and functions that you plan to use, and then write the code.

For this program, we will use two header files. One will control how we handle input and output (stdio.h), and one will allow us to write random numbers (random.h). We'll declare our variables at the top of main() where they can be used throughout our program. The while statement in lines 8-12 is used to read input from the user until enter is pressed, and it stores each value in turnip after separating them with commas. A for loop in lines 16-22 then prints out the number of times each turnip has sprouted, and finally, we end the program with a semicolon.

```
#include <stdio.h>
#include <random.h>
int main() {
// Reads input from the user and stores it in turnip
int A, B, C;
while(inkey( )){

// Save input into variable turnipA, then repeat until
invalidated
```

A = readkey(); // Get next keystroke. if(A == '1'){ // If the user entered 1 print out the max number of sprouts (n) for each turnip. printf("You have {n} sprouts for a total of {n}."); } if(A == '2'){ // If the user entered 2 print out the average number of sprouts (avg) for each turnip.

Chapter 16.

Logging in Programs

Programs are the basic building blocks for coding. Programs can be run without a computer by writing them down on paper, typing them into an online editor, or talking through their steps aloud.

Most programs consist of two parts: (1) telling the computer what you want it to do and (2) instructing the computer on how to do it. The first part is called the command and tells the computer what operations to perform, for example, adding two numbers or erasing a file. The second part is called the instruction method and tells how to perform these operations, e.g., addition or using an erase function in a word processing program.

To begin, you should learn a simple program to introduce the differences between commands and instructions.

Command: "Hello World" (i.e., "Write your name on the screen.")

Instructions: (1) from what line of your program do you write your name, (2) is it centered or justified, and (3) does it have any special formatting?

Commands are one word. They tell the computer what to do. For example, one command might say: "Write your name on the screen." You don't want to worry about how computer memory space is organized or how to format things for output on display! The computer just does them for you. In fact, the computer does all the work for you.

In contrast, instructions tell the computer what to do. For example: "Write your name on the screen." This tells the computer how to make your name appear on the screen. Some instructions require a bit more detail. For example:

(1) from what line of your program do you write your name, (2) is it centered or justified, and (3) does it have any special formatting?
Instructions tell not only what to do but also how to do it! Therefore, they are called "instructions." For example: "Write your name on the screen. Center justified." This tells the computer to:
Write your name Center justified.

There are many kinds of instructions. If you want to add a number, you can write something like this:

number = number + 1 Or you could directly express the instruction like this:
number = number + 1 Write your name Center justified. Add one to the number line.

In programs, it bothers me when you don't write the complete step-by-step procedure in one command or instruction. Instead, each piece of information is usually separated into several more minor instructions called statements. For example, in the examples above, there are two separate instructions: (1) "Write your name" and (2) "Center justified. Write your name." But they are really one statement that you have divided up into smaller pieces.

In code or computer programs, the "commands" and "instruction methods" can be represented as statements or lines of code. Line by line, a program is composed of separate instructions and commands. This is how programs work; one line does one thing.

When you write your programs on paper or type them into an online editor like Notepad++, you should divide up your instructions into multiple steps so that each line has only one instruction. It is important to keep each instruction on a different line of code to show what the computer is doing. For example, if your program has the instruction "Add one to the number line," this is too long to use on one line. Instead, it would be best if you wrote something like this:

number = number + 1

Or if your program has the instruction "Write your name," this is too short of using on one line. Instead, it would help if you wrote something like this:

Write your name, what to do.

When each statement is on a separate line of code, it becomes clear what the computer is doing. Later, when we start writing programs in Python and Ruby, you will learn which command tells the computer what it wants to do, and which lines specify how it does it.

Chapter 17.

Logical Grouping of Programs

-Basic Syntax

-Program Statements

-Line Numbers and Labels

-Optimizing Coding for the Best Possible Practice

-Functions and Procedures

-Arrays and Strings (and Their Relationship to One Another)

-Conditional Execution in Programs

Debugging Programs Without a Debugger - using GDB with GNU Debugger (GDB) (command-line source code debugger) to examine the machine code of compiled programs at run time. Compile your program with debug info, set a breakpoint, and run it. GDB will halt the program at the breakpoint. This walks you through examining all of your program's machine-level details (its source code, including the debug information) and lets you deal with 'live' problems.

The Coding Standard

Coding style is a byproduct of how you view memory, how you view variables, and how you view file I/O. Coding style will make your life easier if it is similar to that which others use. However, coding style may cause aggravation if it differs from that which others use. Basically, there are two ways to approach this: obsess over very small details or err on the side of caution when making changes. Most of us fall somewhere in between, and it's a matter of what works best for you.

The style I tend to use is to use as few curly braces as possible and avoid the occasional parenthesis use. In contrast, most people tend to use every curly brace they can get their hands on and add new parentheses wherever they think they are necessary. There is almost always a way to accomplish what you want without using the unneeded parenthesis. Secondly, never 'parentheses yourself into the ground' with unnecessary brackets and braces unless you (or someone else) have told you that this is necessary for their particular program or library. (It's your life, your choice, but be aware that they are there for a reason.)
Coding Style Examples

The author of this book presents the following example. While not perfect, it comes close. Check out the Wikipedia book on C/AL (C-like syntax) for some excellent examples. I've embedded a link to it further down. The following covers:

"HOTSPOT PLACEMENT" (code hot spot placement)
"VARIABLE NAMES" (variable naming in general), which is relatively brief (one paragraph). It's a small area and worth the mention only.

"MEMORY MANAGEMENT" (code memory management which is seriously flawed)

"PROBLEM EXAMPLE" (code problem example). "Programs that don't exist anymore"

"(a) - Using the pointer a, use a statement to do this. Keep track of what you've done with a variable you could call name. Use that variable's address to store where you are now."

"A - Using the pointer a, do more of this. The program will print out a message about each step it takes. The location should hold the offset to the next line."

"B - Add some code to do this. Pass in a pointer variable called name, and print out the name of each line in the loop (from 1 to n)."
"(b) - Add another method and print out what you've got so far."

"C - Add another loop and use handmade to hide your window from view instead of hiding it from clicks altogether. If the window is 'hidden' with this hot spot, HIDE or SHOW the window."

"D - Add some code to set a hot spot for yourself. Set a hot spot for each of these lines: 1 to n, 1 to n-1, and 1 to n+1."

"E - Start your program again. Go back in time and do it all over again."
"(a) - Create a function. (b) Call it from the main program."
"CODE EXAMPLE" See "Source Code B-01" on page 48 in this source file (here). See also "Source Code B-02" on page 49 in this source file (here).

"Programmers who use this coding style tend to have an elegant and clean code. Their code is almost like that you would see on a good high school math homework problem."

Chapter 18.

Deploying Programs

The internet has revolutionized the way we work, interact, and live. Online tools are used to create, store, and share information with ease. These days, you can use just about any device to code in your own language - learn how to deploy programs online before it's too late!

Thanks to technology's evolution over the past decade or so, these platforms have been developed to save time. You no longer need a degree in computer programming for coding jobs; you can become an online programmer with little-to-no experience whatsoever if you want! Some of these platforms are free, while others charge a fee. For beginners, it is recommended to start with the free platforms first, so you have time to figure out if you want to become a full-time programmer.

The biggest perk of using online coding platforms is that they are accessible from any device. They are also available 24/7, which means that you can work anytime in the day or night when you have an internet connection and know how to code. However, this could also be a disadvantage for those who are looking for part-time jobs; most of these platforms require users to be always online for them to function correctly.
The cons of these platforms are that they tend to be extremely strict when it comes to what can be coded in each platform. While you can use your own code, there will be areas that you cannot access. For example, they might not allow you to create your own games or application. In general, these platforms require a lot of time and dedication before asking for money.

There are several online coding platforms today, all with their pros and cons. Let's look at some of the most popular platforms in 2018:

W3Schools

It is one of the most popular coding platforms today. It has tutorials for beginners and experts alike. The tutorials are available in multiple languages, including English, Spanish, French, German, and Russian. It includes tutorials for all kinds of coding, including web design, web development, and front-end development. W3Schools also provides helpful documentation about code and other computer programming topics in an easy-to-understand manner.

Codecademy

Another great platform that beginners can use to learn how to code is Codecademy. This one features courses for more than 12 languages, including JavaScript, Ruby, HTML/CSS, and PHP. It is best suited for those who are interested in web design or web development. It also has a mobile app, so you can use it anywhere. One of the main advantages of this tutorial is that the interface is easy to understand and use.

Khan Academy

It has courses in over 20 different subjects, including math, science, computer science, history, and many more. A sample of the tutorials includes HTML, CSS, and JavaScript. It is a free learning platform that offers excellent tutorials and support for its users. It is not as easy to use when it comes to coding, but it is a great learning platform nonetheless.

Code Academy

Code Academy has created some of the most effective learning tools in digital programming today. The website features more than 1000 instructional videos on programming for experts and beginners alike. Many of these programs can be used to start a career in computer programming if you know what you are doing. Many schools have also used it to teach students the basics of coding and creating websites. Some of the languages it teaches include Python, PHP, HTML/CSS, JavaScript, Ruby, and Java.

Udemy

Udemy is a great platform to learn how to code online. It features thousands of paid courses that can be taken freely by anyone who wants to learn more about the technical aspects of coding. Some of these courses are free while others cost money. It is one of the biggest platforms when it comes to learning computer programming online. The website also features projects that users have created using different coding languages and platforms around the world. It also offers certification for some topics like Android development. There are plenty of other platforms out there today that you can learn from. It all comes down to what you are looking for in a learning system. If you decide that it is time for you to start pursuing an online career, do not forget to research these coding platforms first. They can help you in your quest to achieve your dreams.

Chapter 19.

Programming for the Internet

Programming for the Internet is a skill that will allow you to create or change the dynamics of any site. How do you decide whether coding for the table is a good idea? If your answer is, "I don't know," then this book is for you! By understanding how programming and computer science works, we'll be able to promote more efficient ways to accomplish our goals. Using some code created by beginners in the past, we'll apply programming fundamentals to an example problem.

One of the most valuable skills for a website owner is making changes to a site. Think about what you do on your site. On many sites, such as blogs and forums, there are options for self-expression and communication with other users. There are also many options for navigation or searching and finding things on your site. On other sites, such as sports forums and news sites, people will schedule games in order to find opponents or books they would like to read.

Some sites need functionality that only a programmer can provide. If you want your site to be able to have more visitors or become more popular, then you'll need the power of programming available from the Table coder (tablecoder.com).

Programming is a broad term that refers to developing programs that are easily understood and executed. For website owners, coding brings the power of modifying or changing a site after it has been created. On many sites, which non-programmers have created in the past, it is easy to change content and functionality without understanding how code works or what makes a particular code more efficient. Other times, you must take the time to understand how things work by trial and error before you'll be able to make your site more valuable.

Programming is one of those specializations that takes many years to master. It requires patience, dedication, and self-education in order to learn the necessary skills needed for success. One of the most important skills you can have is the desire to learn as much as possible. Once you know enough to be able to create your own programs, it will make it easier to donate or sell new functions.

It's Impossible... No Way!

So there are so many websites out there in the world today. It's hard to keep up with all of them. How can you possibly keep track of all the new games, events and groups? How will you ever find something interesting enough to spend time learning about it?

The answer is simple: YOU CAN! You have an opportunity to become a coder for your site. As a coder, you will be able to create functions that change the dynamics of your site. One of the most significant changes you'll make will be in adding plugins that add functionality without knowing how it works. The skills required to become a good coder are established by experience gained in other areas. Coding is more than just writing code with special characters (not that there's anything wrong with that).

What means Programming?

Programming is the process of solving problems with a computer. There are different aspects to programming, but none are more important than the fundamentals of how a computer works and how code can be used in order to control it. This section will focus on the fundamentals when discussing how to use code for your site.

The following image shows an imaginary computer screen. The title at the top reads "Stack Overflow." It is a site that allows programmers to ask questions and solve problems (and give answers, too). The program displayed in this example has many features that help guests find solutions to programming problems.

The computer screen on the right side has a feature called tag clouds. This is a graphical representation of the most popular tags associated with a problem. It's like an index for famous words and phrases used on the site when writing code.
If you're curious to learn more about programming, click here to go to the Stack Overflow site and explore more about Stack Overflow.

Programming Basics: Problem Solving

We'll assume that you have no background in computer science or programming whatsoever. You'll most likely be interested in using the Table coder (http://tablecoder.com) to add features to your site, not necessarily learn how to create a program from scratch. An excellent way to start with programming is by solving problems. It's a powerful tool that can be used in order to accomplish many things. A problem refers to something that needs or should be fixed.

Before you can solve a problem, you need to understand what it is. One of the terms programmers use for understanding something is called "defining the terms." That means that you need to understand exactly what words mean before you'll be able to do anything with them (especially before you can program them).

A computer language uses special characters in order to define the terms for problem-solving and programming. Code is made up of a series of instructions that tell a computer what to do. You can read, write, or change code by using special characters and symbols that we call variables.
The following image represents a desk with papers and pens littered across it. We've organized the papers and pens by color, size and shape. If you want to try this at home:

Start by picking up all the blue pens on your desk (they're probably under your laptop).

Put them back into their place in the box that is labeled "blue." Please pick up all the green pens and put them back in their place as well.
We'll call this the box labeled "green."

After you've picked up all the pens, carefully put them back into their box. It will be easy to see that all the pens are now organized. There's a specific place for each pen and a way to tell which pen belongs were.

Using this method, we can organize anything in our homes or businesses.
We could choose to organize anything from food to furniture or even essential documents from work (like your paycheck). We could also use this system to organize our computer files, like the ones that hold pictures of your family and the important documents from your tax return.

Chapter 20.

Programming for Mobile Devices

Coding is a skill of immense value and interest, but it can seem a daunting task. In this post, we'll go over the basics of coding for mobile devices using HTML5. It's intimidating at first, but once you get to know the language, it can give you access to limitless opportunities...

The Basics: The Language of Code

Coding is often thought of as an exclusive jargon used by expert programmers. However, in reality, they're just using their own language!

Programming languages are simply languages in which people describe how software should function. When people speak English, French, or
Spanish, they're using natural languages. Programming languages are artificial languages whose purpose is to communicate with the software itself. In this post, we'll be using HTML5 to code for mobile devices.

HTML5 is a markup language used in creating web pages. You might already use HTML5 to make your Facebook posts and Twitter messages. This language is used to create websites that all computers (not just mobile ones) can access on the internet. Since it's a standard, you won't ever have to worry about your HTML5 code not working on someone else's device.

The Basics: What is HTML?

HTML stands for Hypertext Markup Language. It's also known as a web markup language or plain old markup language (PLA). It was first created in the nineties and can be seen in many of the online magazines and newspapers on the internet today. You're probably familiar with this language because it's used to create all of those fancy websites, we get to see every day! You might have even written your own basic websites using HTML before...but the basics are just that. Let's get to the juicy stuff!

HTML5 comes with a handful of new features, which allow you to create more interactive websites. We'll only be using a couple of these, but feel free to experiment on your own with the other ones. Another exciting option is CSS3, which we'll be learning about in another post!

Let's Get Started: <!DOCTYPE HTML>

The first thing that you need to know is how to create a primary HTML5 document. Don't panic! To start out, it's easier than you might imagine. HTML5 is a lot simpler to use than HTML4, which takes advantage of more complicated tags and syntax. HTML5 uses semantic tags, which are self-explanatory.
To create a new HTML document, the first line of code that you need to write is:

<!DOCTYPE html>

HTML5 actually comes with several different doctypes (instructions for how the documents are being created). The most universally accepted doctype for creating web pages is the one above. This code has just two letters (html) in all lowercase without any suffixes or prefixes. It just stands as "HTML" to the rest of the world.

When you write it like this, it looks almost like English. This is because HTML5 preserves what other languages call case: upper case letters, capital letter in between two lower case letters, and so on. However, there are some exceptions:

- All cross-references (links) in HTML have < instead of '
. - Proper nouns are capitalized (i.e. Nyan Cat). - Punctuation

marks have their entire character set selected (a handful like the full stop or the question mark). - Emphasis is represented with *asterisks* instead of italics. - Hyphens are used for breaking spaces (e.g.) like 11.*1234*.

Even if you don't follow this exact syntax, you can still use many of the syntax rules it dictates to create websites. The most important one is that every nook and cranny of a webpage should have an appropriate tag identifying what it is. Just as we would speak to each other in English, we turn to language for communication on the internet.

Let's get on with HTML5! The <HEAD> Section

HTML5 makes use of an <head> section, which processes information before the actual document begins to be displayed on a screen. Think of the <head> section like a preface where you list all of the important information about your text. HTML5: The Basics
Let's get started with our first HTML document! This is how the <HEAD> section would look like:

<!DOCTYPE html> <html lang=en> <head> The title of your website should be listed here in both English and in your chosen programming language. </head> </html>
The general convention for writing <title> tags is that it should be capitalized, followed by a space, then its name. This should then go at the top of your webpage (in between the <html></head> tags). If you're attempting to create a mobile website, keep in mind that only the first <title> tag should be used. This will enable your page to have its own unique ID called a Web Title. Since HTML5 has a new way of doing this with a meta tag called "data-web-title=" , it's important that you keep track of this value for future references (you'll be doing this for all the other tags that you'll be using).

The only other important thing to mention is how the title of your webpage works. In HTML4, the concept of "page" was very different from our modern knowledge of it. It referred to what we call today, "web pages". In that case, the title was more of a "title tag", and it was not dependent on the document you were reading.

In HTML5, the Web Title and Page Title are different!

To start with, a Web Title is used to create an identification value that is unique for each page of your website. This is necessary to prevent multiple pages from using the same name (like what might happen if you made a mistake while writing your webpage). For this reason, every web page has its own unique ID (called a web title) which will be listed in the <title> tag. The <title> tag will be placed above the opening <html></head> and before any other content.

Chapter 21.

Difference Between Java, Python and C++

Python is an object-oriented programming language often used for web development or scripting purposes. It is different from other high-level languages like Java and C++ because it mixes procedural and dynamic typing with syntax that resembles English words. On the other hand, Java is a statically typed object-oriented language oriented towards distributed computing systems that web developers can use for server-side applications or system software.

In contrast to Python's English-like syntax, C++ has its own set of rules for declaring variables using keywords such as "int," "float" and "char".
So how do these three programming languages differ from each other? A simple answer would be to state that Python focuses on the code while Java and C++ concentrate on the compiler. Let us briefly analyze this statement in regards to each programming language.

In Python, the code is considered primary and is given more importance than the compiler. For instance, there are no strict rules for naming conventions in Python, unlike Java where all classes have to be named after a class name and its respective package name, e.g. java.util.ArrayList . All that matters in Python is that a class or function is present.

Python recognizes the existence of objects and executes them rather than the syntax. Also, there are no strict rules for indentation in Python, which means that indentations do not affect code execution. A programmer can write code with multiple nested loops and levels of functions without worrying about the number of spaces used in-between.

In Java, on the other hand, compiler rules are considered more important than the code itself which leads to a limited number of things a programmer can do compared to programmers working with Python or C++. In particular, object-oriented programming is emphasized heavily in Java as opposed to procedural programming which is illustrated through C++'s templates and macros features. The way a programmer writes the code is given more importance than the way the code can be executed, leading to confusing Java developers who are used to coding in Python.

In conclusion, Python focuses on the code, Java focuses on compiler rules and C++ focuses on both. In terms of language design, an experienced programmer is better off learning C++ because he/she will be able to understand how a compiler works at a low level but will have problems with learning object-oriented programming in Java. As for an inexperienced programmer looking for a more accessible programming language to learn, Python would be better than Java and C++ because of its short syntax lengths.

Conclusion

Coding is the process of using a computer program (or software) to manipulate data to be used in some applications. It is one form of programming. Programming languages are used to code and program, allowing for more complicated tasks to be completed than by manually writing code by hand. Coding is a crucial part of everyday life for many people worldwide, from business professionals and engineers to designers and those who teach students how to code at school.

Schools are teaching coding to students across the country, and for many reasons. Not only is it a crucial part of modern life, but it allows people to complete tasks more efficiently. It also makes learning how to program computers easier in later years, allowing for skills relevant to future professions. Coding is also an excellent way to encourage students' creativity and problem-solving skills, which will be helpful in many areas of life afterward.

So, what is it about coding that can motivate students? What about the process that can hook them and make them want to learn more? It's really not that hard, fortunately.

Here are some ideas to get you started on your journey into coding, based on my own experiences:

Passion for programming – This may seem like a no-brainer at first, but it's true. For many people, programming is not only a means of achieving a particular goal (such as earning money), but it's also a passion in and of itself. For many people, coding is not only fun but actually makes them happy in the long term. Coding allows students to truly express themselves creatively, both with their code and how they'll create it.

Programming can be very therapeutic for people over long periods.

Real-world application – Many people do not choose an interest in programming simply because it is fun. They do so because they know that it's going to have a real-world application in the future. This is true of almost any academic subject and is undoubtedly true of coding. In fact, many people choose to study a particular course of action purely because they know that their skills will be helpful in the job market or to help them achieve an ideal future career situation. In fact, many students plan to become programmers after graduation as part of a career change.

Creating something interesting and useful – It's much easier to learn something that will have a long-term beneficial purpose than a less useful subject with no reason for learning. Coding is said to provide long-term benefits for those who love it and will help them improve their professional skills in the future.

Coding allows people to create something that they can be proud of. This is incredibly motivating for many students. Since there are no set rules or boundaries in programming, students can get as creative as possible, which means that they can create something exciting and valuable. This is incredibly motivating and exciting for students; after all, that's why they want to learn coding in the first place – mainly because they love making things!